Victoria

A Romantic WEDDING PLANNER

A WELCOME BOOK

HEARST BOOKS
A Division of Sterling Publishing Co., Inc.
NEW YORK

Copyright © 2000 by Welcome Enterprises

All rights reserved.

Produced by Welcome Enterprises, New York
Project Director: Natasha Tabori Fried
Designed by: Lisa Vaughn

All Photography copyright © Hearst Communications, Inc.
Cover (upper left): Wendi Schneider
Cover (upper right): Thomas Hooper
Cover (lower left): Toshi Otsuki
Cover (lower right): Guy Bouchet
Planner & Calendar: (center) Luciana Pampalone; (background) Toshi Otsuki
Celebrations: (center) Steven Randazzo; (background) Richard Dunkley
The Wedding Party: (center) Wendi Schneider; (background) Toshi Otsuki
Guests: (center) Guy Bouchet; (background) Pia Tryde
Music, Flowers, & Photography: (center) Thomas Hooper; (background) Richard W. Brown
Ceremony & Reception: (center) Toshi Otsuki; (background) Toshi Otsuki
The Honeymoon: (center) Theo Gruttman; (background) William P. Steele

Every attempt has been made to obtain permission to reproduce materials protected by copyright. Where omissions have occurred, the producers will be happy to acknowledge this in future printings.

10 9 8 7 6 5 4 3 2

First Paperback Edition 2003
Published by Hearst Books
A Division of Sterling Publishing Co., Inc.
387 Park Avenue South, New York, NY 10016

Hearst Books is proud to continue the superb style, quality, and tradition of Victoria *magazine with every book we publish. On our beautifully illustrated pages you will always find inspiration and ideas about the subjects you love.*

Victoria is a trademark owned by Hearst Magazines Property, Inc., in USA, and Hearst Communications, Inc., in Canada. Hearst Books is a trademark owned by Hearst Communications, Inc.

Distributed in Canada by Sterling Publishing
c/o Canadian Manda Group, One Atlantic Avenue, Suite 105
Toronto, Ontario, Canada M6K 3E7

Distributed in Australia by Capricorn Link (Australia) Pty. Ltd.
P.O. Box 704, Windsor, NSW 2756 Australia

Printed in China

ISBN 1-58816-283-4

Table of Contents

Introduction 6

PLANNER & CALENDAR
Wedding Planner 9
Calendars
- Monthly 12
- Weekly 18
- The Day Before 26
- The Wedding Day 27
- The Day After 28

Budget 30
Newspaper Announcements .. 33
Marriage License 36

CELEBRATIONS
The Engagement Party 39
The Bridal Shower 42
The Rehearsal Dinner 44
The Post-Wedding Brunch ... 49

THE WEDDING PARTY
Participants 53
Division of Duties 58
Accommodations 60
Transportation 62
Beauty Services 64
Wedding Rings 67
Attire
- The Bride 68
- The Bridesmaids 70
- The Groom 71
- The Groomsmen 72
- Child Attendants 73
- Parents 74

GUESTS
Guest List 79

Invitations 104
Accommodations 108
Transportation 109
Gift Registry 110
Wedding Favors 113
Announcement List 114

MUSIC, FLOWERS, & PHOTOGRAPHY
Music
- Ceremony 121
- Reception 122

Flowers
- Ceremony 124
- Reception 125

Photography 127
Videography 128

CEREMONY & RECEPTION
The Ceremony
- Location 131
- Officiant 131
- Vows 134
- Service 135
- Program 136

The Reception
- Location 139
- Rentals 140
- Seating Arrangements 143
- Catering 148
- Beverages 150
- The Wedding Cakes 151

THE HONEYMOON
Personal Information 155
Itinerary 156
Packing List 158

We've been to dozens of weddings over the years. They've varied greatly, but the common thread to every successful wedding has been the bride and groom's attention to the little touches that express their personalities and the specialness of their relationship. Details make a wedding deeply personal, such as adorning the reception tables with your own antique linens, providing each guest room with a surprise basket full of special treats, or wearing your grandmother's lace gown.

You will treasure your wedding day forever, and you want it to be perfect. But a perfect day takes careful planning. Decide together which elements of your wedding mean the most to you—and then make those things your priority. For instance, if your little nieces and nephews will take part in the ceremony, plan a morning or afternoon wedding so that everyone will be wide awake and well-behaved. Or if you always imagined carrying a bridal bouquet of lily of the valley, you'll want to plan a spring wedding. However you choose to personalize your wedding day, your guests will appreciate your efforts.

Planning a wedding should be as much of a joy as the big day itself. This planner is designed to make that possible by helping you record and organize all of your notes, ideas, and estimates. Let it inspire your creativity so that you will experience the wedding you've always dreamed of.

We wish you much happiness, and a wedding day that you will cherish forever.

—Nancy Lindemeyer
Founding Editor, *Victoria* Magazine

He proposed. You said yes. Now what? The coming months will be a lot of fun, but they will also require you to make many decisions, stretch your organizational skills to the maximum, use your best efforts at diplomacy, and through it all be a perfect example of grace under pressure. So before getting wrapped up in the details of planning your wedding, consider more generally what mood and ambience you envision. For inspiration, circle all the words from the list below that you hope will apply to your wedding day.

Elegant	Unique	Romantic
Traditional	Personal	Formal
Extravagant	Casual	Sophisticated
Free-spirited	Intimate	Organized
Simple	Fun	Delicate
Refined	Quiet	Artistic
Loud	Natural	Stylish
Ornate	Tranquil	Joyful

Now ask yourself the following five basic questions:
- What time of year do I want to get married?
- Where do I want to get married?
- Do I want to be married in a house of worship?
- How big a wedding do I want?
- How much money do I want to spend?

If you answered these general questions with decisiveness and clarity, you are already way ahead of the game. Now look at the words you have chosen to describe your wedding and you're ready to begin tackling the details.

Planner & Calendar

Use this wedding planner as your master checklist to remind you of all the decisions you have to make and jobs you must accomplish. Give yourself deadlines, and be realistic about how much you can do on your own. Keeping yourself organized is the key to a smooth and stress-free wedding. And no matter what, remember: You have already found the person you want to spend the rest of your life with. So the hard part is over. Planning your perfect wedding day is just icing on the cake.

The Budget

Many couples aren't sure what they can—or should—spend on their wedding. Because you will treasure the memory of this day for a lifetime, make sure you include the elements that matter most to you. Before you start worrying about the numbers, make a list that includes every likely expense, and then rate each one from most to least important. Once you've decided what matters most, you will find it much easier to compromise on certain elements and hold firm on others. Bear in mind, though, that the old adage "You get what you pay for" is not always true. Sometimes even the simplest (and least costly) details can prove to be a spectacular expression of the love you share for each other.

Newspaper Announcements

Announcing your engagement or wedding in the local paper may seem old-fashioned to a modern bride and groom, but isn't that partly what getting married is all about? Almost everyone enjoys perusing the wedding section on Sunday mornings to see which friends have taken the plunge. It is a nice way to keep family, friends, and business acquaintances alerted to a significant event in your life, without having to send personal announcements to all of them. And besides, it will thrill your grandmother.

♥ ♥ ♥ ♥ ♥

Planner & Calendar

The Wedding Planner

- **6-12 Months (Check when done)**
  - ○ Set a date
  - ○ Make a budget
  - ○ Compile guest list
  - ○ Reserve ceremony location
  - ○ Reserve reception location
  - ○ Order wedding dress and accessories
  - ○ Order groom's attire
  - ○ Choose your attendants
  - ○ Order attendants' attire
  - ○ Send engagement announcement to newspapers
  - ○ Book caterer
  - ○ Book florist
  - ○ Book photographer
  - ○ Book video services
  - ○ Book band and/or DJ for reception
  - ○ Book musicians for ceremony

- **3-6 Months**
  - ○ Finalize guest list
  - ○ Design and order invitations
  - ○ Register for gifts
  - ○ Order wedding rings
  - ○ Book hairdresser and/or makeup artist
  - ○ Order wedding cake
  - ○ Make honeymoon reservations
  - ○ Arrange accommodations for wedding night
  - ○ Arrange accommodations for out-of-town guests
  - ○ Purchase gifts for attendants
  - ○ Purchase party favors for guests
  - ○ Reserve tent and lighting equipment
  - ○ Confirm delivery date of dress

- **3 Months**
  - ○ Mail invitations
  - ○ Meet with officiant to discuss ceremony
  - ○ Finalize menu with caterer
  - ○ Finalize floral arrangements with florist
  - ○ Select song list with band
  - ○ Select music for ceremony

Planner & Calendar

- ○ Schedule portraits with photographer
- ○ Schedule beauty treatments
- ○ Reserve rental equipment for ceremony and reception
- ○ Arrange wedding day transportation
- ○ Schedule ceremony rehearsal
- ○ Schedule rehearsal dinner
- ○ Schedule day-after gathering
- ○ Schedule physical and blood tests

2 Months
- ○ Write vows
- ○ Purchase guest book
- ○ Send wedding announcement to newspapers
- ○ Pick up wedding dress and bridesmaids' dresses
- ○ Pick up shoes and accessories
- ○ Pick up wedding rings
- ○ Finalize ceremony schedule
- ○ Finalize reception schedule

1 Month
- ○ Arrange seating for reception
- ○ Review reception and ceremony schedule with all services
- ○ Rehearse personal vows
- ○ Practice makeup and hair
- ○ Pick up marriage license

1–2 Weeks
- ○ Confirm final head count with caterer
- ○ Write place cards
- ○ Address wedding announcements
- ○ Pack for honeymoon

Day Before
- ○ Mail wedding announcements
- ○ Give attendants gifts
- ○ Rehearse ceremony
- ○ Rehearsal dinner

Wedding Day
- ○ Run through personal vows
- ○ Schedule plenty of time to get ready
- ○ Breathe!

| Planner & Calendar |

NOTES

| Planner & Calendar |

Month: _____ 20_____

Sunday	Monday	Tuesday	Wednesday	Thursday	Friday	Saturday

Month: _____ 20_____

Sunday	Monday	Tuesday	Wednesday	Thursday	Friday	Saturday

Planner & Calendar

Month: _____ 20_____

Sunday	Monday	Tuesday	Wednesday	Thursday	Friday	Saturday

Month: _____ 20_____

Sunday	Monday	Tuesday	Wednesday	Thursday	Friday	Saturday

Planner & Calendar

Month: _____ 20 _____

Sunday	Monday	Tuesday	Wednesday	Thursday	Friday	Saturday

Month: _____ 20 _____

Sunday	Monday	Tuesday	Wednesday	Thursday	Friday	Saturday

Planner & Calendar

Month: _____ 20 _____

Sunday	Monday	Tuesday	Wednesday	Thursday	Friday	Saturday

Month: _____ 20 _____

Sunday	Monday	Tuesday	Wednesday	Thursday	Friday	Saturday

| Planner & Calendar |

Month: _____ 20_____

Sunday	Monday	Tuesday	Wednesday	Thursday	Friday	Saturday

Month: _____ 20_____

Sunday	Monday	Tuesday	Wednesday	Thursday	Friday	Saturday

|Planner & Calendar|

Month: _____ 20_____

Sunday	Monday	Tuesday	Wednesday	Thursday	Friday	Saturday

Month: _____ 20_____

Sunday	Monday	Tuesday	Wednesday	Thursday	Friday	Saturday

| Planner & Calendar |

Week of: _____   20_____

Sunday

Monday

Tuesday

Wednesday

Thursday

Friday

Saturday

| Planner & Calendar |

Week of: _____ 20_____

Sunday

Monday

Tuesday

Wednesday

Thursday

Friday

Saturday

| Planner & Calendar |

Week of: _____   20 _____

Sunday

Monday

Tuesday

Wednesday

Thursday

Friday

Saturday

| Planner & Calendar |

Week of: _____   20_____

Sunday

Monday

Tuesday

Wednesday

Thursday

Friday

Saturday

| Planner & Calendar |

Week of: _____   20_____

Sunday

Monday

Tuesday

Wednesday

Thursday

Friday

Saturday

| Planner & Calendar |

WEEK OF: _____ 20_____

Sunday

Monday

Tuesday

Wednesday

Thursday

Friday

Saturday

| Planner & Calendar |

Week of: _____   20_____

Sunday

Monday

Tuesday

Wednesday

Thursday

Friday

Saturday

| *Planner & Calendar* |

WEEK OF: _____   20_____

Sunday

Monday

Tuesday

Wednesday

Thursday

Friday

Saturday

| Planner & Calendar |

THE DAY BEFORE   DATE: _____

6:00 A.M.
_____

7:00 A.M.
_____

8:00 A.M.
_____

9:00 A.M.
_____

10:00 A.M.
_____

11:00 A.M.
_____

12:00 P.M.
_____

1:00 P.M.
_____

2:00 P.M.
_____

3:00 P.M.
_____

4:00 P.M.
_____

5:00 P.M.
_____

6:00 P.M.
_____

7:00 P.M.
_____

8:00 P.M.
_____

9:00 P.M.
_____

| Planner & Calendar |

The Wedding Day   Date: _____

6:00 A.M.
_____

7:00 A.M.
_____

8:00 A.M.
_____

9:00 A.M.
_____

10:00 A.M.
_____

11:00 A.M.
_____

12:00 P.M.
_____

1:00 P.M.
_____

2:00 P.M.
_____

3:00 P.M.
_____

4:00 P.M.
_____

5:00 P.M.
_____

6:00 P.M.
_____

7:00 P.M.
_____

8:00 P.M.
_____

9:00 P.M.
_____

| *Planner & Calendar* |

THE DAY AFTER   DATE: _____

6:00 A.M.
_____

7:00 A.M.
_____

8:00 A.M.
_____

9:00 A.M.
_____

10:00 A.M.
_____

11:00 A.M.
_____

12:00 P.M.
_____

1:00 P.M.
_____

2:00 P.M.
_____

3:00 P.M.
_____

4:00 P.M.
_____

5:00 P.M.
_____

6:00 P.M.
_____

7:00 P.M.
_____

8:00 P.M.
_____

9:00 P.M.
_____

| Planner & Calendar |

NOTES

| *Planner & Calendar* |

The Budget

		Estimated Cost	Final Cost
Ceremony:	Location fee	_____	_____
	Rental equipment	_____	_____
	Officiant's fee	_____	_____
	Printed programs	_____	_____
Reception:	Location fee	_____	_____
	Rental equipment	_____	_____
	Tent rental	_____	_____
	Lighting rental	_____	_____
Catering:	Food	_____	_____
	Service	_____	_____
Wedding cake		_____	_____
Beverages		_____	_____
Flowers and decorations:	Ceremony flowers	_____	_____
	Reception flowers	_____	_____
	Bouquets and boutonnieres	_____	_____
Photography		_____	_____
Videography		_____	_____
Music:	Reception band/DJ	_____	_____
	Ceremony musicians	_____	_____
Transportation		_____	_____
Beauty services		_____	_____
Wedding bands		_____	_____

| Planner & Calendar |

The Budget

	Estimated Cost	Final Cost
Wedding-night accommodations	_____	_____
Marriage license	_____	_____
The wedding dress	_____	_____
Shoes and accessories	_____	_____
The groom's attire	_____	_____
Invitations	_____	_____
Announcements	_____	_____
Guest accommodations	_____	_____
Wedding favors	_____	_____
Attendants' gifts	_____	_____
Engagement party	_____	_____
Rehearsal dinner	_____	_____
Day-after brunch	_____	_____
Honeymoon	_____	_____

Miscellaneous:

_____

_____

_____

TOTAL: _____ _____

Planner & Calendar

Notes

Expenses

Although many modern brides and grooms share the cost of the wedding, convention dictates that the bride's family assumes the majority of the expenses. Customarily, the groom and his family pay only for the honeymoon, the rings, the groom's attire, the ceremonial bouquets and boutonnieres, the officiant's fee, the rehearsal dinner, the marriage license, and blood test, if necessary.

Newspaper Announcements

Engagement Announcement

Publication: _____ Contact: _____
Address: _____
_____

Phone: _____ Fax: _____ E-mail: _____
Due date: _____ Cost: _____
Text: _____
_____
_____
_____
_____
_____
_____
_____
_____

Publication: _____ Contact: _____
Address: _____
_____

Phone: _____ Fax: _____ E-mail: _____
Due date: _____ Cost: _____
Text: _____
_____
_____
_____
_____
_____
_____
_____
_____

Planner & Calendar

Newspaper Announcements

❦ Wedding Announcement

Publication: _____ Contact: _____
Address: _____
_____

Phone: _____ Fax: _____ E-mail: _____
Due date: _____ Cost: _____
Text: _____
_____
_____
_____
_____
_____
_____
_____

Publication: _____ Contact: _____
Address: _____
_____

Phone: _____ Fax: _____ E-mail: _____
Due date: _____ Cost: _____
Text: _____
_____
_____
_____
_____
_____
_____
_____

| *Planner & Calendar* |

NOTES

Planner & Calendar

Marriage License

Contact: _____

Address: _____
_____

Phone: _____ Fax: _____ E-mail: _____

Required documentation: _____
_____
_____
_____

Fee: _____

Notes: _____
_____
_____
_____
_____
_____
_____
_____
_____
_____
_____
_____
_____
_____
_____

The Wedding License

*D*ifferent states have varying laws on how far ahead of time you must apply for a wedding license. Check with your local City Hall for details on what your state requires to issue the license, which may include: a blood test, different forms of identification, proof of address, and your nuptial date.

Celebrations

One of the best things about getting married is having an excuse to throw a variety of parties. Engagement parties, bridal showers, bachelor parties, bachelorette parties, rehearsal dinners, and day-after brunches have all grown in popularity in recent years. These celebrations give you more time to spend time with guests and loved ones, since the wedding itself is often such a whirlwind for the bride and groom.

The Engagement Party

Engagement parties are a great way to bring together all your friends and family to celebrate your decision to get married. Often, a close relative throws this event for the bride and groom as a gift. An engagement party can range from elegant and formal to relaxed and casual, depending on personal preference. If cost is an issue, keep it simple. Consider, for instance, making it a cocktail party and serve only hors d'oeuvres, wine, and champagne. Invitations can easily be handmade with a friend, and decorations can be as minimal as candles and bud vases filled with single roses or greenery. Often, the simplest events leave the strongest impressions.

The Bridal Shower & Bachelor Party

Fortunately, these are the two events for which the bride and groom are not responsible—aside from providing a guest list, if necessary.

Though anyone can host the bridal shower, it is traditionally thrown by the maid of honor, with help from the bridesmaids. Some brides may have more than one, in order to make life more convenient for her guests. Bridal showers used to be very tame affairs, where the bride received contributions to her hope chest from her female friends over tea or lemonade and cookies. But these days, there are many different ways to have a bridal shower. They can have themes, such as "kitchen," "the honeymoon," or "lingerie." Guests may be asked ahead of time to contribute to a commemorative token for the bride, such as favorite recipes that can make up a recipe box or scrapbook pages to recall her single life. Showers can also incorporate the traditional, such as using the ribbons from the shower gifts to fashion a bouquet the bride will use for her wedding rehearsal.

The bachelor party is usually a very different type of celebration. Only the groom, his male attendants, and other friends attend. No gifts are involved. When the best man gets creative, these events can turn into weekends where the guys take a trip together, fishing, skiing, hiking, etc. Some of his friends might also want to make a home video about the groom, which can be shown at the party.

The Rehearsal Dinner & Post-Wedding Shower

Many weddings include events the night before and the morning after the ceremony and reception. These social functions give the bride and groom and their families an opportunity to spend quality time with all their guests, many of whom may have traveled a long distance to attend. Consider serving special foods to make these events unique and different from the wedding itself. For example, a Maine wedding might call for a lobster bake as the rehearsal dinner, while a Texas wedding party may dictate a southern barbecue. These festivities also offer great opportunities to incorporate family traditions. If, for instance, your fiancé's family belongs to a different ethnicity or religion, consider honoring them with an event that incorporates their heritage.

Whether you lean toward the traditional or opt for the more unconventional, these added celebrations can greatly enrich the memory of your wedding for you and your loved ones.

♥ ♥ ♥ ♥ ♥ ♥

Celebrations

The Engagement Party

Host: _____
Date: _____ Time: _____
Address: _____
Phone: _____ Fax: _____ E-mail: _____

❧ Flowers
Florist: _____ Contact: _____
Address: _____
Phone: _____ Fax: _____ E-mail: _____
Flowers ordered: _____
_____
_____ Cost: _____

❧ Food & Beverages
Caterer: _____ Contact: _____
Address: _____
Phone: _____ Fax: _____ E-mail: _____
Menu: _____
_____
_____
_____ Cost: _____
Beverages: _____
_____
_____ Cost: _____

❧ Rentals
Rental company: _____ Contact: _____
Address: _____
Phone: _____ Fax: _____ E-mail: _____
Rentals: _____
_____
_____ Cost: _____

Engagement Party Guest List

Name(s)   Gift   Thank-you sent

ENGAGEMENT PARTY GUEST LIST

Name(s)   Gift   Thank-you sent

Celebrations

The Bridal Shower

Hostess: _____ Date: _____ Time: _____
Address: _____
Phone: _____ Fax: _____ E-mail: _____

Bridal Shower Guest List

Name(s)	Gift	Thank-you sent
		○
		○
		○
		○
		○
		○
		○
		○
		○
		○
		○
		○
		○
		○
		○
		○
		○
		○
		○
		○
		○
		○
		○
		○
		○
		○

Celebrations

BRIDAL SHOWER GUEST LIST

Name(s)　　　　　　　　　　　　Gift　　　　　　　　　　　　Thank-you sent

Celebrations

The Rehearsal Dinner

Host: _____

Location: _____ Cost: _____

Date: _____ Time: _____

Address: _____

Phone: _____ Fax: _____ E-mail: _____

❧ Flowers

Florist: _____ Contact: _____

Address: _____

Phone: _____ Fax: _____ E-mail: _____

Flowers ordered: _____

_____

_____ Cost: _____

❧ Food & Beverages

Caterer: _____ Contact: _____

Address: _____

Phone: _____ Fax: _____ E-mail: _____

Menu: _____

_____

_____ Cost: _____

Beverages: _____

_____

_____ Cost: _____

❧ Rentals

Rental company: _____ Contact: _____

Address: _____

Phone: _____ Fax: _____ E-mail: _____

Rentals: _____

_____

_____ Cost: _____

Celebrations

Rehearsal Dinner Guest List

Celebrations

Rehearsal Dinner Seating Arrangements

Table #1
1. _____
2. _____
3. _____
4. _____
5. _____
6. _____
7. _____
8. _____
9. _____
10. _____

Table #2
1. _____
2. _____
3. _____
4. _____
5. _____
6. _____
7. _____
8. _____
9. _____
10. _____

Table #3
11. _____
2. _____
3. _____
4. _____
5. _____
6. _____
7. _____
8. _____
9. _____
10. _____

Table #4
1. _____
2. _____
3. _____
4. _____
5. _____
6. _____
7. _____
8. _____
9. _____
10. _____

Table #5
11. _____
2. _____
3. _____
4. _____
5. _____
6. _____
7. _____
8. _____
9. _____
10. _____

Table #6
1. _____
2. _____
3. _____
4. _____
5. _____
6. _____
7. _____
8. _____
9. _____
10. _____

Celebrations

Rehearsal Dinner Seating Arrangements

Table #7
1. _____
2. _____
3. _____
4. _____
5. _____
6. _____
7. _____
8. _____
9. _____
10. _____

Table #8
1. _____
2. _____
3. _____
4. _____
5. _____
6. _____
7. _____
8. _____
9. _____
10. _____

Table #9
11. _____
2. _____
3. _____
4. _____
5. _____
6. _____
7. _____
8. _____
9. _____
10. _____

Table #10
1. _____
2. _____
3. _____
4. _____
5. _____
6. _____
7. _____
8. _____
9. _____
10. _____

Table #11
11. _____
2. _____
3. _____
4. _____
5. _____
6. _____
7. _____
8. _____
9. _____
10. _____

Table #12
1. _____
2. _____
3. _____
4. _____
5. _____
6. _____
7. _____
8. _____
9. _____
10. _____

Use this space to sketch the table arrangement.

Celebrations

The Post-Wedding Brunch or Breakfast

Host: _____
Location: _____ Cost: _____
Date: _____ Time: _____
Address: _____
Phone: _____ Fax: _____ E-mail: _____

❧ Flowers

Florist: _____ Contact: _____
Address: _____
Phone: _____ Fax: _____ E-mail: _____
Flowers ordered: _____
_____
_____ Cost: _____

❧ Food & Beverages

Caterer: _____ Contact: _____
Address: _____
Phone: _____ Fax: _____ E-mail: _____
Menu: _____
_____
_____ Cost: _____
Beverages: _____
_____
_____ Cost: _____

❧ Rentals

Rental company: _____ Contact: _____
Address: _____
Phone: _____ Fax: _____ E-mail: _____
Rentals: _____
_____
_____ Cost: _____

NOTES & ESTIMATES

The bridesmaids and groomsmen

are usually chosen from among the couple's closest friends and relatives. It is considered a great honor and responsibility to be asked to attend a loved one at their wedding. In particular, the maid of honor and the best man often play important roles in the preparations and ceremony.

The maid of honor traditionally hosts the bridal shower a few months before the wedding, and assists the bride in choosing her dress and the attendants' dresses. She also helps the bride prepare on her wedding day and looks after her personal belongings, such as gloves or a hand purse. During the procession, the maid of honor is the last bridesmaid to walk down the aisle. Throughout the ceremony, she stands closest to the bride and holds her bouquet whenever necessary. The bride might also ask her maid of honor to keep tissues on hand, just in case. At the reception, it is common for the maid of honor to toast the newlyweds.

The best man, as we all know, hosts the bachelor party. Traditionally an all-male event celebrating the groom's last days as a single man, the bachelor party is attended by all the groom's attendants and other male friends. The best man also helps the groom choose his wedding wardrobe and his attendants' wardrobe. On the wedding day, the best man keeps the groom company as he prepares, and holds the wedding bands until they are requested in the ceremony. At the altar, he stands just to the side of the groom and escorts the maid of honor down the aisle. He is often called upon to toast the happy couple at the reception.

Other attendants, including bridesmaids and ushers, may be asked to assume certain duties. Planning a wedding can be an enormous responsibility, and most family members and friends, especially the attendants, are more than happy to pitch in and help out. So don't be shy about requesting help and delegating responsibility—your friends and loved ones will consider it a privilege.

Wedding Attire

Every bride has fantasized about her wedding day, often since childhood, when she first heard the fairy tales of *Cinderella* or *Sleeping Beauty*. At the center of these daydreams is the wedding dress, the delicate gown that transforms every young woman into an extraordinary beauty.

The wedding gown should be nothing less than your idea of perfection. It ought to set the tone of your entire wedding. For this reason, it should be the first choice you make, perhaps even before the ceremony and reception locations. Pick a dress that makes you feel both special and comfortable, that embodies your fantasies and gives you goose bumps when you first slip it over your head in the dressing room. You may only wear it once in your lifetime, but it will be unforgettable, to you, your husband, and all your guests.

Creating your wedding around your dress gives you the freedom to pick the style you love the most, without worrying about whether it fits the season or the setting of the ceremony. Let the dress dictate all the other details, such as the kind of flowers, music, and location. If you don't have the luxury of buying the dress before committing to a date and place, at least give your fantasy dress serious thought first. For instance, if your heart is set on wearing a ball-gown, resist the temptation to get married on the beach, and consider where such a dress would feel most at home.

Though many grooms may not become heavily involved in the planning of their wedding, choosing their wardrobe is often the exception. Without giving away the details of your dress, you should let your fiancé know its general style so that he can select an outfit that is complementary. The groomsmen's and bridesmaids' attire should also be in keeping with the bride's dress. Accessories, such as shoes, jewelry, gloves, and a veil, may be decided upon later. Take care to select accessories that subtly accentuate, rather than distract from, the beauty of the dress.

♥ ♥ ♥ ♥ ♥

The Wedding Party

Participants

❧ Maid of Honor
Name: _____
Address: _____
Phone: _____ Fax: _____ E-mail: _____
Notes: _____
_____

❧ Bridesmaids
Name: _____
Address: _____
Phone: _____ Fax: _____ E-mail: _____
Notes: _____

Name: _____
Address: _____
Phone: _____ Fax: _____ E-mail: _____
Notes: _____

Name: _____
Address: _____
Phone: _____ Fax: _____ E-mail: _____
Notes: _____

Name: _____
Address: _____
Phone: _____ Fax: _____ E-mail: _____
Notes: _____

Name: _____
Address: _____
Phone: _____ Fax: _____ E-mail: _____
Notes: _____

The Wedding Party

Participants

Name: _____
Address: _____
Phone: _____ Fax: _____ E-mail: _____
Notes: _____

Name: _____
Address: _____
Phone: _____ Fax: _____ E-mail: _____
Notes: _____

Name: _____
Address: _____
Phone: _____ Fax: _____ E-mail: _____
Notes: _____

❧ Best Man

Name: _____
Address: _____
Phone: _____ Fax: _____ E-mail: _____
Notes: _____

❧ Ushers

Name: _____
Address: _____
Phone: _____ Fax: _____ E-mail: _____
Notes: _____

Name: _____
Address: _____
Phone: _____ Fax: _____ E-mail: _____
Notes: _____

The Wedding Party

Participants

Name: _____
Address: _____
Phone: _____ Fax: _____ E-mail: _____
Notes: _____

Name: _____
Address: _____
Phone: _____ Fax: _____ E-mail: _____
Notes: _____

Name: _____
Address: _____
Phone: _____ Fax: _____ E-mail: _____
Notes: _____

Name: _____
Address: _____
Phone: _____ Fax: _____ E-mail: _____
Notes: _____

Name: _____
Address: _____
Phone: _____ Fax: _____ E-mail: _____
Notes: _____

Name: _____
Address: _____
Phone: _____ Fax: _____ E-mail: _____
Notes: _____

The Wedding Party

PARTICIPANTS

❦ Child Attendants

Name: _____
Parents: _____
Address: _____
Phone: _____ Fax: _____ E-mail: _____

Name: _____
Parents: _____
Address: _____
Phone: _____ Fax: _____ E-mail: _____

Name: _____
Parents: _____
Address: _____
Phone: _____ Fax: _____ E-mail: _____

Name: _____
Parents: _____
Address: _____
Phone: _____ Fax: _____ E-mail: _____
Notes: _____

Flower Girls

*M*any young flower girls may experience stage fright or a reluctance to walk down the aisle on the day of the wedding. Making them feel comfortable around you and your groom ahead of time may help avoid wedding day jitters. Try to schedule a few play dates with your younger attendants in the months before the wedding. Most little girls love the "dressing up" part of being in a wedding, and it helps to involve them in choosing their dresses so that they feel comfortable in what they're wearing. And make sure they have ample time to rehearse!

The Wedding Party

Participants

❧ Mother of the Bride
Name: _____
Address: _____
Phone: _____ Fax: _____ E-mail: _____
Notes: _____
_____

❧ Father of the Bride
Name: _____
Address: _____
Phone: _____ Fax: _____ E-mail: _____
Notes: _____
_____

❧ Mother of the Groom
Name: _____
Address: _____
Phone: _____ Fax: _____ E-mail: _____
Notes: _____
_____

❧ Father of the Groom
Name: _____
Address: _____
Phone: _____ Fax: _____ E-mail: _____
Notes: _____
_____

❧ Other
Name: _____
Address: _____
Phone: _____ Fax: _____ E-mail: _____
Notes: _____
_____

# The Wedding Party

Division of Duties

Task	Performed by	Done
		○

The Wedding Party

Division of Duties

Task	Performed by	Done
		○

The Wedding Party

Accommodations ❧ The Bride & Groom

❧ Before the Wedding (bride)

Hotel: _____ Contact: _____
Address: _____
Phone: _____ Fax: _____ E-mail: _____
Room #: _____ Rate: _____
Check-in time: _____ Checkout time: _____
Directions: _____
_____
_____
_____

❧ Before the Wedding (groom)

Hotel: _____ Contact: _____
Address: _____
Phone: _____ Fax: _____ E-mail: _____
Room #: _____ Rate: _____
Check-in time: _____ Checkout time: _____
Directions: _____
_____
_____
_____

❧ After the Wedding

Hotel: _____ Contact: _____
Address: _____
Phone: _____ Fax: _____ E-mail: _____
Room #: _____ Rate: _____
Check-in time: _____ Checkout time: _____
Directions: _____
_____
_____
_____

The Wedding Party

ACCOMMODATIONS ❦ THE WEDDING PARTY

Hotel: _____ Contact: _____
Address: _____
Phone: _____ Fax: _____ E-mail: _____
Rate: _____
Check-in time: _____ Checkout time: _____

Name	Room #	Arrival Date	Departure Date

Directions: _____
_____
_____

The Wedding Party

Transportation

Vehicle service/rental: _____ Contact: _____
Address: _____
Phone: _____ Fax: _____ E-mail: _____
Number of vehicles and drivers: _____
Cost: _____

❧ Before the Wedding

Directions to ceremony: _____
_____
_____

Passenger	Pickup time	Pickup Location	Confirmation #

❧ After the Wedding

Directions from ceremony to reception: _____
_____
_____

Passenger	Pickup time	Pickup Location	Confirmation #

The Wedding Party

NOTES & ESTIMATES

Transportation

*D*on't forget to give careful thought to the transportation needs of both you and your wedding guests. If, for instance, the ceremony and reception locations are far from each other, a detailed map or car service should be provided for each guest. Make sure you book the newlyweds' transportation to arrive at least fifteen minutes before the scheduled end of the ceremony, and remember to arrange for guest parking ahead of time.

The Wedding Party

BEAUTY SERVICES

❖ Hair & Makeup

Salon: _____
Address: _____
Phone: _____ Fax: _____ E-mail: _____

Hair stylist: _____
Appointments:

Name	Time	Cost

Makeup artist: _____
Appointments:

Name	Time	Cost

❖ Manicure/Pedicure

Salon: _____
Address: _____
Phone: _____ Fax: _____ E-mail: _____

The Wedding Party

Beauty Services

Manicurist: _____

Appointments:

Name	Service	Time	Cost
_____	_____	_____	_____
_____	_____	_____	_____
_____	_____	_____	_____
_____	_____	_____	_____
_____	_____	_____	_____
_____	_____	_____	_____
_____	_____	_____	_____

Other Services

Salon: _____ Contact: _____
Address: _____
Phone: _____ Fax: _____ E-mail: _____
Services being performed: _____
_____
_____

Cost: _____
Time(s) of appointment(s): _____
_____

Salon: _____ Contact: _____
Address: _____
Phone: _____ Fax: _____ E-mail: _____
Services being performed: _____
_____
_____

Cost: _____
Time(s) of appointment(s): _____
_____

The Wedding Party

Notes & Estimates

The Wedding Party

WEDDING RINGS

Purchased from: _____

Salesperson: _____

Address: _____

Phone: _____ Fax: _____ E-mail: _____

Description of rings: _____

_____

_____

Cost of groom's ring: _____

Cost of bride's ring: _____

Delivery date: _____

Engraving: _____

_____

_____

_____

Special instructions: _____

_____

_____

_____

_____

_____

_____

_____

Tradition

The ritual of the groom carrying his bride over the threshold for the first time as a married couple dates back to pagan times. It was believed that evil spirits gathered at the entrance of a home, and so the bride was held aloft to avoid being touched by the dark apparitions. Today, this custom is thought to bring good fortune to the newlywed couple.

The Wedding Party

Attire ❧ The Bride

❧ Wedding dress

Purchased from: _____ Salesperson: _____
Address: _____
Phone: _____ Fax: _____ E-mail: _____
Designer: _____
Size: _____ Color: _____ Style#: _____
Cost: _____ Date of delivery: _____
Accessories: _____
_____
_____
_____

Fitting schedule:
Date   Time
_____
_____
_____

❧ Shoes

Purchased from: _____ Salesperson: _____
Address: _____
Phone: _____ Fax: _____ E-mail: _____
Designer: _____
Size: _____ Color: _____ Style#: _____
Cost: _____ Date of delivery: _____

❧ Undergarments

Purchased from: _____ Salesperson: _____
Address: _____
Phone: _____ Fax: _____ E-mail: _____
Designer: _____
Size: _____ Color: _____ Style#: _____
Cost: _____ Date of delivery: _____

The Wedding Party

NOTES & ESTIMATES

Bridesmaids' Dresses

If you're having difficulty finding one dress that looks flattering on all your attendants, consider letting them select their own outfits. Provide them with general guidelines for style and color, or have them all buy their dresses in white and dye them to match.

The Wedding Party

Attire ❧ The Bridesmaids

❧ Dresses

Purchased from: _____ Salesperson: _____
Address: _____
Phone: _____ Fax: _____ E-mail: _____
Designer: _____
Size(s): _____
Color: _____ Style#: _____
Cost: _____ Date of delivery: _____
Items/accessories purchased: _____
_____
_____
_____

Fitting schedule:

Bridesmaid	Size	Date	Time

❧ Shoes

Purchased from: _____ Salesperson: _____
Address: _____
Phone: _____ Fax: _____ E-mail: _____
Designer: _____
Size(s): _____
Color: _____ Style#: _____
Cost: _____ Date of delivery: _____
Notes: _____
_____

The Wedding Party

Attire ❦ The Groom

❦ Ceremony Attire

Purchased from: _____ Salesperson: _____

Address: _____

Phone: _____ Fax: _____ E-mail: _____

Designer: _____

Size: _____ Color: _____ Style#: _____

Cost: _____ Date of delivery: _____

Items purchased/rented: _____

_____
_____
_____
_____
_____

Fitting schedule:

Date   Time

_____
_____
_____
_____

Notes: _____

_____
_____
_____
_____
_____
_____
_____
_____

The Wedding Party

Attire ❧ The Groomsmen

❧ Ceremony Attire

Purchased from: _____ Salesperson: _____
Address: _____
Phone: _____ Fax: _____ E-mail: _____
Designer: _____
Size(s): _____
Color: _____ Style#: _____
Cost: _____ Date of delivery: _____
Items purchased/rented: _____
_____
_____
_____
_____
_____

Fitting schedule:

Groomsman	Size	Date	Time

Notes: _____
_____
_____
_____

The Wedding Party

Attire ❧ Child Attendants

❧ Ceremony Attire

Purchased from: _____ Salesperson: _____
Address: _____
Phone: _____ Fax: _____ E-mail: _____
Designer: _____
Size(s): _____
Color: _____ Style#: _____
Cost: _____ Date of delivery: _____
Items purchased: _____
_____
_____
_____

Fitting schedule:

Attendant	Size	Date	Time
_____	_____	_____	_____
_____	_____	_____	_____
_____	_____	_____	_____
_____	_____	_____	_____

Notes: _____
_____
_____
_____

The Guest Book

*I*nstead of placing your guest book at the exit of the ceremonial venue, where guests may feel rushed as they pass through the receiving line, consider assigning your flower girls or a few young guests to take the book around to each table during the reception. Not only will this give each guest time to write a meaningful message, but it is a wonderful way to keep the children at your wedding occupied and give them a sense of importance.

The Wedding Party

Attire ❦ Parents of the Bride

❦ Mother of the Bride

Purchased from: _____ Salesperson: _____
Address: _____
Phone: _____ Fax: _____ E-mail: _____
Designer: _____
Size: _____ Color: _____ Style#: _____
Cost: _____ Date of delivery: _____
Accessories: _____
_____
_____

Fitting schedule:

Date   Time
_____
_____
_____
_____

❦ Father of the Bride

Purchased from: _____ Salesperson: _____
Address: _____
Phone: _____ Fax: _____ E-mail: _____
Designer: _____
Size: _____ Color: _____ Style#: _____
Cost: _____ Date of delivery: _____
Items purchased/rented: _____
_____

Fitting schedule:

Date   Time
_____
_____
_____

The Wedding Party

Attire ❧ Parents of the Groom

❧ Mother of the Groom
Purchased from:_____ Salesperson:_____
Address:_____
Phone:_____ Fax:_____ E-mail:_____
Designer:_____
Size:_____ Color:_____ Style#:_____
Cost:_____ Date of delivery:_____
Accessories:_____
_____
_____

Fitting schedule:
Date   Time
_____
_____
_____
_____

❧ Father of the Groom
Purchased from:_____ Salesperson:_____
Address:_____
Phone:_____ Fax:_____ E-mail:_____
Designer:_____
Size:_____ Color:_____ Style#:_____
Cost:_____ Date of delivery:_____
Items purchased/rented:_____
_____
_____

Fitting schedule:
Date   Time
_____
_____
_____

The Wedding Party

Notes & Estimates

Deciding on a guest list early on will help you tackle other important choices more easily, such as location, food, transportation, accommodations, and ordering the invitations.

Your guest list will largely depend on the style of wedding you prefer and the size of the ceremony and reception locations. If you've always dreamed of an intimate ceremony on the beach, you may want to consider inviting just your immediate family and friends. If the wedding is to be a large one, then the task of deciding whom to invite becomes much simpler. Remember, anyone who is not invited to the wedding can still be sent a wedding announcement.

Use the guest list section to keep a careful record of who has been mailed an invitation, who has sent an RSVP, and the gift they give you. If you write thank-you notes for gifts as they arrive rather than waiting to do them all at once, you'll find the process much easier. Personal notes are an absolute must and mean a great deal to the recipients. Another way to show your guests how much you appreciate their attendance is to give them a small wedding favor they can keep as a momento of your wedding. Popular wedding favors include monogrammed objects such as votive candle holders, champagne glasses, handkerchiefs, paperweights, or picture frames. Edible treats, such as a small box of chocolates or an organza bag filled with silver-coated almonds, are most traditional party favors. Other ideas might include placing bud vases filled with flowers or silver-framed place cards at each table-setting for guests to take home as keepsakes. Consider also giving a living gift, such a single narcissus bulb nestled in a small ceramic pot or glass bowl, or a beautiful sachet of wildflower seeds.

Invitations should reflect the style of your wedding, both in design and language. Usually, the more traditional the wedding the more formal the invitations ought to be. Before choosing the phrasing for your invitation, look through the stationer's or printer's sample books for ideas. In addition to the invitation card you may wish to add any of the following enclosures: a reply card and stamped return envelope, tissue paper, confetti, satin ribbon, a map, travel directions, hotel contact information, or a photograph of the engaged couple. (It is always considerate to send out-of-town guests a few options in accommodation that vary in price.) If you plan to hold the wedding at a remote location or wish to invite a large number of out-of-town guests, invitations should be sent out as early as six to twelve weeks before. Otherwise, four to six weeks is the traditional advance notice.

Most stationers offer printing options that vary in price and style. The most expensive is engraving, which results in raised typeface on one side and indented type on the other. Thermography is a less costly printing process that also results in a raised type, but without leaving any indentation. The least expensive method is offset lithography, often used for business cards or stationery. All three are considered tasteful, and the choice depends on your personal taste and budget.

Gift Registry

Registering for wedding gifts is a wonderful way to let your friends and family know what you need and want for your new home together. Some couples register only at one location, usually a department store that sells kitchenware, china, linens, and appliances. But it has become increasingly common to register at a few different shops, each specializing in a particular area. You may also elect to register for wedding gifts on-line. A number of sites offer this service and can be easily located by doing an internet search. Most registry websites offer a large selection of different retailers, which allows you the added convenience of keeping your registry in one location.

♥ ♥ ♥ ♥ ♥

Guests

The Guest List

Name(s): _____
Address: _____
Phone: _____ Fax: _____ E-mail: _____
Number of guests attending: _____ Accommodations: _____
Travel itinerary: _____
_____

Gift received: _____ Thank-you note sent: _____

Name(s): _____
Address: _____
Phone: _____ Fax: _____ E-mail: _____
Number of guests attending: _____ Accommodations: _____
Travel itinerary: _____
_____

Gift received: _____ Thank-you note sent: _____

Name(s): _____
Address: _____
Phone: _____ Fax: _____ E-mail: _____
Number of guests attending: _____ Accommodations: _____
Travel itinerary: _____
_____

Gift received: _____ Thank-you note sent: _____

Name(s): _____
Address: _____
Phone: _____ Fax: _____ E-mail: _____
Number of guests attending: _____ Accommodations: _____
Travel itinerary: _____
_____

Gift received: _____ Thank-you note sent: _____

The Guest List

Name(s): _____
Address: _____
Phone: _____ Fax: _____ E-mail: _____
Number of guests attending: _____ Accommodations: _____
Travel itinerary: _____
_____
Gift received: _____ Thank-you note sent: _____

Name(s): _____
Address: _____
Phone: _____ Fax: _____ E-mail: _____
Number of guests attending: _____ Accommodations: _____
Travel itinerary: _____
_____
Gift received: _____ Thank-you note sent: _____

Name(s): _____
Address: _____
Phone: _____ Fax: _____ E-mail: _____
Number of guests attending: _____ Accommodations: _____
Travel itinerary: _____
_____
Gift received: _____ Thank-you note sent: _____

Name(s): _____
Address: _____
Phone: _____ Fax: _____ E-mail: _____
Number of guests attending: _____ Accommodations: _____
Travel itinerary: _____
_____
Gift received: _____ Thank-you note sent: _____

Guests

The Guest List

Name(s): _____
Address: _____
Phone: _____ Fax: _____ E-mail: _____
Number of guests attending: _____ Accommodations: _____
Travel itinerary: _____
_____
Gift received: _____ Thank-you note sent: _____

Name(s): _____
Address: _____
Phone: _____ Fax: _____ E-mail: _____
Number of guests attending: _____ Accommodations: _____
Travel itinerary: _____
_____
Gift received: _____ Thank-you note sent: _____

Name(s): _____
Address: _____
Phone: _____ Fax: _____ E-mail: _____
Number of guests attending: _____ Accommodations: _____
Travel itinerary: _____
_____
Gift received: _____ Thank-you note sent: _____

Name(s): _____
Address: _____
Phone: _____ Fax: _____ E-mail: _____
Number of guests attending: _____ Accommodations: _____
Travel itinerary: _____
_____
Gift received: _____ Thank-you note sent: _____

The Guest List

Name(s): _____
Address: _____
Phone: _____ Fax: _____ E-mail: _____
Number of guests attending: _____ Accommodations: _____
Travel itinerary: _____
_____
Gift received: _____ Thank-you note sent: _____

Name(s): _____
Address: _____
Phone: _____ Fax: _____ E-mail: _____
Number of guests attending: _____ Accommodations: _____
Travel itinerary: _____
_____
Gift received: _____ Thank-you note sent: _____

Name(s): _____
Address: _____
Phone: _____ Fax: _____ E-mail: _____
Number of guests attending: _____ Accommodations: _____
Travel itinerary: _____
_____
Gift received: _____ Thank-you note sent: _____

Name(s): _____
Address: _____
Phone: _____ Fax: _____ E-mail: _____
Number of guests attending: _____ Accommodations: _____
Travel itinerary: _____
_____
Gift received: _____ Thank-you note sent: _____

Guests

The Guest List

Name(s): _____
Address: _____
Phone: _____ Fax: _____ E-mail: _____
Number of guests attending: _____ Accommodations: _____
Travel itinerary: _____
_____

Gift received: _____ Thank-you note sent: _____

Name(s): _____
Address: _____
Phone: _____ Fax: _____ E-mail: _____
Number of guests attending: _____ Accommodations: _____
Travel itinerary: _____
_____

Gift received: _____ Thank-you note sent: _____

Name(s): _____
Address: _____
Phone: _____ Fax: _____ E-mail: _____
Number of guests attending: _____ Accommodations: _____
Travel itinerary: _____
_____

Gift received: _____ Thank-you note sent: _____

Name(s): _____
Address: _____
Phone: _____ Fax: _____ E-mail: _____
Number of guests attending: _____ Accommodations: _____
Travel itinerary: _____
_____

Gift received: _____ Thank-you note sent: _____

The Guest List

Name(s): _____
Address: _____
Phone: _____ Fax: _____ E-mail: _____
Number of guests attending: _____ Accommodations: _____
Travel itinerary: _____
_____
Gift received: _____ Thank-you note sent: _____

Name(s): _____
Address: _____
Phone: _____ Fax: _____ E-mail: _____
Number of guests attending: _____ Accommodations: _____
Travel itinerary: _____
_____
Gift received: _____ Thank-you note sent: _____

Name(s): _____
Address: _____
Phone: _____ Fax: _____ E-mail: _____
Number of guests attending: _____ Accommodations: _____
Travel itinerary: _____
_____
Gift received: _____ Thank-you note sent: _____

Name(s): _____
Address: _____
Phone: _____ Fax: _____ E-mail: _____
Number of guests attending: _____ Accommodations: _____
Travel itinerary: _____
_____
Gift received: _____ Thank-you note sent: _____

Guests

The Guest List

Name(s): _____

Address: _____

Phone: _____ Fax: _____ E-mail: _____

Number of guests attending: _____ Accommodations: _____

Travel itinerary: _____
_____

Gift received: _____ Thank-you note sent: _____

Name(s): _____

Address: _____

Phone: _____ Fax: _____ E-mail: _____

Number of guests attending: _____ Accommodations: _____

Travel itinerary: _____
_____

Gift received: _____ Thank-you note sent: _____

Name(s): _____

Address: _____

Phone: _____ Fax: _____ E-mail: _____

Number of guests attending: _____ Accommodations: _____

Travel itinerary: _____
_____

Gift received: _____ Thank-you note sent: _____

Name(s): _____

Address: _____

Phone: _____ Fax: _____ E-mail: _____

Number of guests attending: _____ Accommodations: _____

Travel itinerary: _____
_____

Gift received: _____ Thank-you note sent: _____

The Guest List

Name(s): _____
Address: _____
Phone: _____ Fax: _____ E-mail: _____
Number of guests attending: _____ Accommodations: _____
Travel itinerary: _____
_____

Gift received: _____ Thank-you note sent: _____

Name(s): _____
Address: _____
Phone: _____ Fax: _____ E-mail: _____
Number of guests attending: _____ Accommodations: _____
Travel itinerary: _____
_____

Gift received: _____ Thank-you note sent: _____

Name(s): _____
Address: _____
Phone: _____ Fax: _____ E-mail: _____
Number of guests attending: _____ Accommodations: _____
Travel itinerary: _____
_____

Gift received: _____ Thank-you note sent: _____

Name(s): _____
Address: _____
Phone: _____ Fax: _____ E-mail: _____
Number of guests attending: _____ Accommodations: _____
Travel itinerary: _____
_____

Gift received: _____ Thank-you note sent: _____

Guests

The Guest List

Name(s): _____
Address: _____
Phone: _____ Fax: _____ E-mail: _____
Number of guests attending: _____ Accommodations: _____
Travel itinerary: _____
_____
Gift received: _____ Thank-you note sent: _____

Name(s): _____
Address: _____
Phone: _____ Fax: _____ E-mail: _____
Number of guests attending: _____ Accommodations: _____
Travel itinerary: _____
_____
Gift received: _____ Thank-you note sent: _____

Name(s): _____
Address: _____
Phone: _____ Fax: _____ E-mail: _____
Number of guests attending: _____ Accommodations: _____
Travel itinerary: _____
_____
Gift received: _____ Thank-you note sent: _____

Name(s): _____
Address: _____
Phone: _____ Fax: _____ E-mail: _____
Number of guests attending: _____ Accommodations: _____
Travel itinerary: _____
_____
Gift received: _____ Thank-you note sent: _____

The Guest List

Name(s): _____
Address: _____
Phone: _____ Fax: _____ E-mail: _____
Number of guests attending: _____ Accommodations: _____
Travel itinerary: _____
_____
Gift received: _____ Thank-you note sent: _____

Name(s): _____
Address: _____
Phone: _____ Fax: _____ E-mail: _____
Number of guests attending: _____ Accommodations: _____
Travel itinerary: _____
_____
Gift received: _____ Thank-you note sent: _____

Name(s): _____
Address: _____
Phone: _____ Fax: _____ E-mail: _____
Number of guests attending: _____ Accommodations: _____
Travel itinerary: _____
_____
Gift received: _____ Thank-you note sent: _____

Name(s): _____
Address: _____
Phone: _____ Fax: _____ E-mail: _____
Number of guests attending: _____ Accommodations: _____
Travel itinerary: _____
_____
Gift received: _____ Thank-you note sent: _____

Guests

The Guest List

Name(s): _____
Address: _____
Phone: _____ Fax: _____ E-mail: _____
Number of guests attending: _____ Accommodations: _____
Travel itinerary: _____
_____
Gift received: _____ Thank-you note sent: _____

Name(s): _____
Address: _____
Phone: _____ Fax: _____ E-mail: _____
Number of guests attending: _____ Accommodations: _____
Travel itinerary: _____
_____
Gift received: _____ Thank-you note sent: _____

Name(s): _____
Address: _____
Phone: _____ Fax: _____ E-mail: _____
Number of guests attending: _____ Accommodations: _____
Travel itinerary: _____
_____
Gift received: _____ Thank-you note sent: _____

Name(s): _____
Address: _____
Phone: _____ Fax: _____ E-mail: _____
Number of guests attending: _____ Accommodations: _____
Travel itinerary: _____
_____
Gift received: _____ Thank-you note sent: _____

The Guest List

Name(s): _____
Address: _____
Phone: _____ Fax: _____ E-mail: _____
Number of guests attending: _____ Accommodations: _____
Travel itinerary: _____
_____

Gift received: _____ Thank-you note sent: _____

Name(s): _____
Address: _____
Phone: _____ Fax: _____ E-mail: _____
Number of guests attending: _____ Accommodations: _____
Travel itinerary: _____
_____

Gift received: _____ Thank-you note sent: _____

Name(s): _____
Address: _____
Phone: _____ Fax: _____ E-mail: _____
Number of guests attending: _____ Accommodations: _____
Travel itinerary: _____
_____

Gift received: _____ Thank-you note sent: _____

Name(s): _____
Address: _____
Phone: _____ Fax: _____ E-mail: _____
Number of guests attending: _____ Accommodations: _____
Travel itinerary: _____
_____

Gift received: _____ Thank-you note sent: _____

Guests

The Guest List

Name(s): _____

Address: _____

Phone: _____ Fax: _____ E-mail: _____

Number of guests attending: _____ Accommodations: _____

Travel itinerary: _____
_____

Gift received: _____ Thank-you note sent: _____

Name(s): _____

Address: _____

Phone: _____ Fax: _____ E-mail: _____

Number of guests attending: _____ Accommodations: _____

Travel itinerary: _____
_____

Gift received: _____ Thank-you note sent: _____

Name(s): _____

Address: _____

Phone: _____ Fax: _____ E-mail: _____

Number of guests attending: _____ Accommodations: _____

Travel itinerary: _____
_____

Gift received: _____ Thank-you note sent: _____

Name(s): _____

Address: _____

Phone: _____ Fax: _____ E-mail: _____

Number of guests attending: _____ Accommodations: _____

Travel itinerary: _____
_____

Gift received: _____ Thank-you note sent: _____

Guests

The Guest List

Name(s): _____
Address: _____
Phone: _____ Fax: _____ E-mail: _____
Number of guests attending: _____ Accommodations: _____
Travel itinerary: _____
_____
Gift received: _____ Thank-you note sent: _____

Name(s): _____
Address: _____
Phone: _____ Fax: _____ E-mail: _____
Number of guests attending: _____ Accommodations: _____
Travel itinerary: _____
_____
Gift received: _____ Thank-you note sent: _____

Name(s): _____
Address: _____
Phone: _____ Fax: _____ E-mail: _____
Number of guests attending: _____ Accommodations: _____
Travel itinerary: _____
_____
Gift received: _____ Thank-you note sent: _____

Name(s): _____
Address: _____
Phone: _____ Fax: _____ E-mail: _____
Number of guests attending: _____ Accommodations: _____
Travel itinerary: _____
_____
Gift received: _____ Thank-you note sent: _____

Guests

The Guest List

Name(s): _____
Address: _____
Phone: _____ Fax: _____ E-mail: _____
Number of guests attending: _____ Accommodations: _____
Travel itinerary: _____
_____

Gift received: _____ Thank-you note sent: _____

Name(s): _____
Address: _____
Phone: _____ Fax: _____ E-mail: _____
Number of guests attending: _____ Accommodations: _____
Travel itinerary: _____
_____

Gift received: _____ Thank-you note sent: _____

Name(s): _____
Address: _____
Phone: _____ Fax: _____ E-mail: _____
Number of guests attending: _____ Accommodations: _____
Travel itinerary: _____
_____

Gift received: _____ Thank-you note sent: _____

Name(s): _____
Address: _____
Phone: _____ Fax: _____ E-mail: _____
Number of guests attending: _____ Accommodations: _____
Travel itinerary: _____
_____

Gift received: _____ Thank-you note sent: _____

The Guest List

Name(s): _____
Address: _____
Phone: _____ Fax: _____ E-mail: _____
Number of guests attending: _____ Accommodations: _____
Travel itinerary: _____
_____
Gift received: _____ Thank-you note sent: _____

Name(s): _____
Address: _____
Phone: _____ Fax: _____ E-mail: _____
Number of guests attending: _____ Accommodations: _____
Travel itinerary: _____
_____
Gift received: _____ Thank-you note sent: _____

Name(s): _____
Address: _____
Phone: _____ Fax: _____ E-mail: _____
Number of guests attending: _____ Accommodations: _____
Travel itinerary: _____
_____
Gift received: _____ Thank-you note sent: _____

Name(s): _____
Address: _____
Phone: _____ Fax: _____ E-mail: _____
Number of guests attending: _____ Accommodations: _____
Travel itinerary: _____
_____
Gift received: _____ Thank-you note sent: _____

Guests

The Guest List

Name(s): _____
Address: _____
Phone: _____ Fax: _____ E-mail: _____
Number of guests attending: _____ Accommodations: _____
Travel itinerary: _____
_____
Gift received: _____ Thank-you note sent: _____

Name(s): _____
Address: _____
Phone: _____ Fax: _____ E-mail: _____
Number of guests attending: _____ Accommodations: _____
Travel itinerary: _____
_____
Gift received: _____ Thank-you note sent: _____

Name(s): _____
Address: _____
Phone: _____ Fax: _____ E-mail: _____
Number of guests attending: _____ Accommodations: _____
Travel itinerary: _____
_____
Gift received: _____ Thank-you note sent: _____

Name(s): _____
Address: _____
Phone: _____ Fax: _____ E-mail: _____
Number of guests attending: _____ Accommodations: _____
Travel itinerary: _____
_____
Gift received: _____ Thank-you note sent: _____

The Guest List

Name(s): _____
Address: _____
Phone: _____ Fax: _____ E-mail: _____
Number of guests attending: _____ Accommodations: _____
Travel itinerary: _____
_____
Gift received: _____ Thank-you note sent: _____

Name(s): _____
Address: _____
Phone: _____ Fax: _____ E-mail: _____
Number of guests attending: _____ Accommodations: _____
Travel itinerary: _____
_____
Gift received: _____ Thank-you note sent: _____

Name(s): _____
Address: _____
Phone: _____ Fax: _____ E-mail: _____
Number of guests attending: _____ Accommodations: _____
Travel itinerary: _____
_____
Gift received: _____ Thank-you note sent: _____

Name(s): _____
Address: _____
Phone: _____ Fax: _____ E-mail: _____
Number of guests attending: _____ Accommodations: _____
Travel itinerary: _____
_____
Gift received: _____ Thank-you note sent: _____

Guests

The Guest List

Name(s): _____

Address: _____

Phone: _____ Fax: _____ E-mail: _____

Number of guests attending: _____ Accommodations: _____

Travel itinerary: _____
_____

Gift received: _____ Thank-you note sent: _____

Name(s): _____

Address: _____

Phone: _____ Fax: _____ E-mail: _____

Number of guests attending: _____ Accommodations: _____

Travel itinerary: _____
_____

Gift received: _____ Thank-you note sent: _____

Name(s): _____

Address: _____

Phone: _____ Fax: _____ E-mail: _____

Number of guests attending: _____ Accommodations: _____

Travel itinerary: _____
_____

Gift received: _____ Thank-you note sent: _____

Name(s): _____

Address: _____

Phone: _____ Fax: _____ E-mail: _____

Number of guests attending: _____ Accommodations: _____

Travel itinerary: _____
_____

Gift received: _____ Thank-you note sent: _____

The Guest List

Name(s): _____
Address: _____
Phone: _____ Fax: _____ E-mail: _____
Number of guests attending: _____ Accommodations: _____
Travel itinerary: _____
_____
Gift received: _____ Thank-you note sent: _____

Name(s): _____
Address: _____
Phone: _____ Fax: _____ E-mail: _____
Number of guests attending: _____ Accommodations: _____
Travel itinerary: _____
_____
Gift received: _____ Thank-you note sent: _____

Name(s): _____
Address: _____
Phone: _____ Fax: _____ E-mail: _____
Number of guests attending: _____ Accommodations: _____
Travel itinerary: _____
_____
Gift received: _____ Thank-you note sent: _____

Name(s): _____
Address: _____
Phone: _____ Fax: _____ E-mail: _____
Number of guests attending: _____ Accommodations: _____
Travel itinerary: _____
_____
Gift received: _____ Thank-you note sent: _____

Guests

The Guest List

Name(s): _____
Address: _____
Phone: _____ Fax: _____ E-mail: _____
Number of guests attending: _____ Accommodations: _____
Travel itinerary: _____
_____
Gift received: _____ Thank-you note sent: _____

Name(s): _____
Address: _____
Phone: _____ Fax: _____ E-mail: _____
Number of guests attending: _____ Accommodations: _____
Travel itinerary: _____
_____
Gift received: _____ Thank-you note sent: _____

Name(s): _____
Address: _____
Phone: _____ Fax: _____ E-mail: _____
Number of guests attending: _____ Accommodations: _____
Travel itinerary: _____
_____
Gift received: _____ Thank-you note sent: _____

Name(s): _____
Address: _____
Phone: _____ Fax: _____ E-mail: _____
Number of guests attending: _____ Accommodations: _____
Travel itinerary: _____
_____
Gift received: _____ Thank-you note sent: _____

The Guest List

Name(s): _____
Address: _____
Phone: _____ Fax: _____ E-mail: _____
Number of guests attending: _____ Accommodations: _____
Travel itinerary: _____
_____
Gift received: _____ Thank-you note sent: _____

Name(s): _____
Address: _____
Phone: _____ Fax: _____ E-mail: _____
Number of guests attending: _____ Accommodations: _____
Travel itinerary: _____
_____
Gift received: _____ Thank-you note sent: _____

Name(s): _____
Address: _____
Phone: _____ Fax: _____ E-mail: _____
Number of guests attending: _____ Accommodations: _____
Travel itinerary: _____
_____
Gift received: _____ Thank-you note sent: _____

Name(s): _____
Address: _____
Phone: _____ Fax: _____ E-mail: _____
Number of guests attending: _____ Accommodations: _____
Travel itinerary: _____
_____
Gift received: _____ Thank-you note sent: _____

Guests

The Guest List

Name(s): _____
Address: _____
Phone: _____ Fax: _____ E-mail: _____
Number of guests attending: _____ Accommodations: _____
Travel itinerary: _____
_____
Gift received: _____ Thank-you note sent: _____

Name(s): _____
Address: _____
Phone: _____ Fax: _____ E-mail: _____
Number of guests attending: _____ Accommodations: _____
Travel itinerary: _____
_____
Gift received: _____ Thank-you note sent: _____

Name(s): _____
Address: _____
Phone: _____ Fax: _____ E-mail: _____
Number of guests attending: _____ Accommodations: _____
Travel itinerary: _____
_____
Gift received: _____ Thank-you note sent: _____

Name(s): _____
Address: _____
Phone: _____ Fax: _____ E-mail: _____
Number of guests attending: _____ Accommodations: _____
Travel itinerary: _____
_____
Gift received: _____ Thank-you note sent: _____

The Guest List

Name(s): _____
Address: _____
Phone: _____ Fax: _____ E-mail: _____
Number of guests attending: _____ Accommodations: _____
Travel itinerary: _____
_____
Gift received: _____ Thank-you note sent: _____

Name(s): _____
Address: _____
Phone: _____ Fax: _____ E-mail: _____
Number of guests attending: _____ Accommodations: _____
Travel itinerary: _____
_____
Gift received: _____ Thank-you note sent: _____

Name(s): _____
Address: _____
Phone: _____ Fax: _____ E-mail: _____
Number of guests attending: _____ Accommodations: _____
Travel itinerary: _____
_____
Gift received: _____ Thank-you note sent: _____

Name(s): _____
Address: _____
Phone: _____ Fax: _____ E-mail: _____
Number of guests attending: _____ Accommodations: _____
Travel itinerary: _____
_____
Gift received: _____ Thank-you note sent: _____

NOTES & ESTIMATES

INVITATIONS

❦ The Stationery

Stationer: _____ Contact: _____
Address: _____
Phone: _____ Fax: _____ E-mail: _____
Quantity: _____
Description: _____
_____
_____
Cost: _____
Delivery date: _____
Notes & estimates: _____
_____
_____
_____
_____
_____
_____
_____

A Courtesy for Out of Town Guests

*P*roviding "Welcome baskets" for out-of-town guests is a lovely gesture to show your appreciation for the distance they've traveled to join you on your wedding day. Baskets might contain any of the following items:

- ❦ A map of the area
- ❦ Delicious snacks such as nuts or chocolate
- ❦ A contact list for the wedding party and other friends
- ❦ A scented candle
- ❦ A handkerchief
- ❦ A list of local sites of interest
- ❦ Travel-size toiletries
- ❦ A disposable camera
- ❦ A deck of playing cards
- ❦ A popular magazine
- ❦ Bottled water

INVITATIONS

❥ The Content
Use this space to compose the content of your invitation.

| Guests |

INSIDE: INVITATIONS

❧ The Design
Below are samples of a traditional wedding invitation and more casual options.

Mr. & Mrs. Victor O'Halloran
Request the honor of your presence
at the marriage of their daughter
Jane O'Halloran
to
Mr. Alexander Fisher
Saturday, the 10th of January
Two Thousand and One
at half after six o'clock
Trinity Cathedral
New York, New York

Black Tie

You are joyously invited
to the wedding celebration of
Alexander Fisher & Jane O'Halloran

Sunday, May 14th, 2003
at 11 o'clock am
Little Chapel
Point Reys, CA

Feast & merriment to follow!

Alexander Fisher &
Jane O'Halloran
together
with their families request
the pleasure of your company in
the celebration of their marriage.
Friday, January 11, 2003
8 o'clock pm
River Boat Club
New Orleans, Louisiana
Dinner & Dancing to follow.

Jane O'Halloran
AND
Alexander Fisher

WOULD BE HONORED TO HAVE YOU
SHARE IN THE JOY OF THEIR MARRIAGE

SATURDAY, JUNE 2ND, 2001
4:00 PM
THE LAKESIDE LODGE
BLACK BUTTE, OREGON

| *Guests* |

INVITATIONS

❦ The Design

Before you consult a stationer, use this space to sketch out how you would like your invitations to look. Having some idea of what you want will make it easier to select from a variety of choices.

Accommodations

Hotel: _____ Contact: _____
Address: _____
Phone: _____ Fax: _____ E-mail: _____
Special rates? Yes ○ $ _____ No ○ $ _____
Amenities & restrictions: _____
_____

Directions: _____
_____
_____
_____

Notes: _____
_____
_____
_____
_____
_____

Hotel: _____ Contact: _____
Address: _____
Phone: _____ Fax: _____ E-mail: _____
Special rates? Yes ○ $ _____ No ○ $ _____
Amenities & restrictions: _____
_____

Directions: _____
_____
_____
_____

Notes: _____
_____
_____
_____
_____

Guests

Accommodations

Hotel: _____ Contact: _____

Address: _____

Phone: _____ Fax: _____ E-mail: _____

Special rates? Yes ○ $ _____ No ○ $ _____

Amenities & Restrictions: _____
_____

Directions: _____
_____
_____
_____

Notes: _____
_____
_____
_____
_____

❧ Transportation/shuttle

Vehicle service/rental: _____ Contact: _____

Address: _____

Phone: _____ Fax: _____ E-mail: _____

Number of vehicles and drivers: _____

Cost: _____

Pickup time(s)   Pickup   Drop-off
_____
_____
_____
_____
_____

Directions: _____
_____
_____

| *Guests* |

Gift Registry

Store: _____ Contact: _____
Address: _____
Phone: _____ Fax: _____ E-mail: _____
Registry list:

| Item | Brand & style # | Price |

_____
_____
_____
_____
_____
_____
_____
_____
_____
_____
_____
_____
_____
_____
_____
_____
_____
_____
_____
_____
_____
_____
_____
_____

Gift Registry

Store: _____ Contact: _____

Address: _____

Phone: _____ Fax: _____ E-mail: _____

Registry list:

Item   Brand & style #   Price

_____
_____
_____
_____
_____
_____
_____
_____
_____
_____
_____
_____
_____
_____
_____
_____
_____
_____
_____
_____
_____
_____
_____
_____
_____

| *Guests* |

Gift Registry

Store: _____ Contact: _____
Address: _____
Phone: _____ Fax: _____ E-mail: _____
Registry list:
Item					Brand & Style #			Price
_____
_____
_____
_____
_____
_____
_____
_____
_____
_____
_____
_____
_____
_____
_____
_____
_____
_____
_____
_____
_____
_____
_____
_____
_____
_____

Wedding Favors

Purchased from: _____ Contact: _____
Address: _____
Phone: _____ Fax: _____ E-mail: _____
Gifts purchased: _____
_____
_____
_____
_____
_____

Number of gifts: _____
Cost: _____ Delivery date: _____
Notes & estimates: _____
_____
_____
_____
_____
_____
_____
_____
_____

Tradition

*A*n old Polish wedding tradition dictates that for good luck, the bride's mother present her daughter with an apron decorated with symbols of fertility and domesticity, such as pacifiers and cooking utensils. Though inappropriate for many of today's brides, this ritual could be modernized creatively by depicting elements of the bride's interests and passions, like her career and hobbies, on a sweater or shirt. If handcrafted with love and humor, such a personal article of clothing could be kept forever as a special reminder of the wedding day.

The Announcement List

Name(s): _____
Address: _____
Relationship to bride or groom: _____

Name(s): _____
Address: _____
Relationship to bride or groom: _____

Name(s): _____
Address: _____
Relationship to bride or groom: _____

Name(s): _____
Address: _____
Relationship to bride or groom: _____

Name(s): _____
Address: _____
Relationship to bride or groom: _____

Name(s): _____
Address: _____
Relationship to bride or groom: _____

Wedding Announcements

Many couples who opt for a smaller wedding choose to send out wedding announcements to those who were not invited as a courtesy. Even in the case of a larger wedding, announcements may also be mailed to professional associates and acquaintances of the bride or groom and their families.

The Announcement List

Name(s): _____
Address: _____
Relationship to bride or groom: _____

Name(s): _____
Address: _____
Relationship to bride or groom: _____

Name(s): _____
Address: _____
Relationship to bride or groom: _____

Name(s): _____
Address: _____
Relationship to bride or groom: _____

Name(s): _____
Address: _____
Relationship to bride or groom: _____

Name(s): _____
Address: _____
Relationship to bride or groom: _____

Name(s): _____
Address: _____
Relationship to bride or groom: _____

Name(s): _____
Address: _____
Relationship to bride or groom: _____

THE ANNOUNCEMENT LIST

Name(s): _____
Address: _____
Relationship to bride or groom: _____

Name(s): _____
Address: _____
Relationship to bride or groom: _____

Name(s): _____
Address: _____
Relationship to bride or groom: _____

Name(s): _____
Address: _____
Relationship to bride or groom: _____

Name(s): _____
Address: _____
Relationship to bride or groom: _____

Name(s): _____
Address: _____
Relationship to bride or groom: _____

Name(s): _____
Address: _____
Relationship to bride or groom: _____

Name(s): _____
Address: _____
Relationship to bride or groom: _____

Guests

The Announcement List

Name(s): _____
Address: _____
Relationship to bride or groom: _____

Name(s): _____
Address: _____
Relationship to bride or groom: _____

Name(s): _____
Address: _____
Relationship to bride or groom: _____

Name(s): _____
Address: _____
Relationship to bride or groom: _____

Name(s): _____
Address: _____
Relationship to bride or groom: _____

Name(s): _____
Address: _____
Relationship to bride or groom: _____

Name(s): _____
Address: _____
Relationship to bride or groom: _____

Name(s): _____
Address: _____
Relationship to bride or groom: _____

Guests

The Announcement List

Name(s): _____
Address: _____
Relationship to bride or groom: _____

Name(s): _____
Address: _____
Relationship to bride or groom: _____

Name(s): _____
Address: _____
Relationship to bride or groom: _____

Name(s): _____
Address: _____
Relationship to bride or groom: _____

Name(s): _____
Address: _____
Relationship to bride or groom: _____

Name(s): _____
Address: _____
Relationship to bride or groom: _____

Name(s): _____
Address: _____
Relationship to bride or groom: _____

Name(s): _____
Address: _____
Relationship to bride or groom: _____

Music, Flowers, & Photography

Think of the music as a soundtrack to your wedding. Choosing a twenty-piece orchestra or a five-member jazz ensemble will greatly influence the general mood of the event. Consider the size of your reception and ceremony locations before deciding on the style of the band and number of musicians. After all, you don't want people shouting over the music to speak to one another during dinner or straining to hear the beat as they take to the dance floor.

There are certainly many styles of music available, including any combination of the following: big band, rhythm and blues, classical, country, disco, jazz, reggae, rock, and swing. Referrals from friends and acquaintances are usually the most successful way to find a good band. If possible, try to see them play live at another event before booking them, or at least ask them to submit a tape. Another option is to hire a DJ to play recorded music.

More than just providing overall ambience, music can also be used to offset and accentuate important moments during your ceremony and reception. Give your band or DJ a list of songs you would like played throughout the evening and for particular events.

Flowers

Flowers will help set the mood for your wedding. Your choice of blooms might suggest elegance (roses, orchids, or calla lilies) or country casual (tulips, wild flowers, or daisies). So can your choice of colors. A cluster of red or dark pink roses, for example, is more formal than an arrangement of blush roses mixed with pale peonies and delphinium.

In addition to traditional table centerpieces and ceremonial bouquets, flowers can be used in a variety of ways to decorate the reception and ceremony locations. Garlands can be wrapped around poles and pillars or fastened to pews and hung along the walls of a room. Larger arrangements in urns or pots can define entryways or be placed on either side of the altar. A single stem placed at each table setting adds an elegant touch, while a spray of flowers attached to the back of the newlyweds' chairs announces with style that they are the guests of honor. Small potted plants can line paths or stairways, and rose petals can be used to shower the bride and groom as a substitute for rice or birdseed. These are only a handful of ideas for using flowers and greenery for your wedding. Consult with your florist and ask to see photos of his or her previous work for inspiration.

Photography

Selecting a good photographer is one of the most important decisions you will make for your wedding. In addition to your personal memories and perhaps a video, the pictures taken at your wedding will be an important reminder of the events and emotions of the day. What style do you prefer? Journalistic or traditional, black and white, or color? Some couples hire two photographs for their wedding, one to shoot formal color portraits, and one to shoot more casual pictures—perhaps even black-and-white for a different effect.

Consider, too, the personality of the photographer who will be sharing some of the most intimate moments of your life at close proximity. It's very important you feel comfortable in his or her presence. Ask prospective candidates for a number of referrals, and be sure you understand the way their estimate works; some photographers quote an all-inclusive price while others will charge a package fee that includes only contact sheets, with prints costing extra. You can also supplement their work by placing disposable cameras on each table and asking your guests to take pictures of their own!

♥ ♥ ♥ ♥ ♥ ♥

| Music, Flowers, & Photography |

Music

❦ Ceremony

Band/Company: _____ Contact: _____
Address: _____
Phone: _____ Fax: _____ E-mail: _____
Time booked: _____ Cost: _____

Music & Song requests:

Activity	Song or music selection
Prelude	_____
Processional	_____
Bride's entrance	_____
Hymnals	_____
Recessional	_____
Receiving line	_____
Other	_____
_____	_____
_____	_____
_____	_____
_____	_____
_____	_____
_____	_____
_____	_____

Choosing the Music

*T*he music you select for your ceremony and reception, whether live or recorded, might be anything from highly traditional wedding music, to songs that reflect your own taste. Your organist and bandleader can be tremendous resources for you when it comes to choosing the music for these occasions. Set up a time to sit down with them several months before your wedding and discuss your options and their recommendations.

Music, Flowers, & Photography

Music

❧ Reception

Band or DJ: _____ Contact: _____

Address: _____

Phone: _____ Fax: _____ E-mail: _____

Time booked: _____ Cost: _____

Music & Song requests:

Activity	Song or music selection
First dance	_____
Bride's dance with her father	_____
Cutting the cake	_____
Throwing the bouquet	_____
Last dance	_____

Other particular dances or special requests

_____   _____
_____   _____
_____   _____
_____   _____
_____   _____
_____   _____

Notes:
_____
_____
_____
_____
_____
_____
_____
_____

Music, Flowers, & Photography

Notes & Estimates

Music, Flowers, & Photography

FLOWERS

Florist: _____ Contact: _____
Address: _____
Phone: _____ Fax: _____ E-mail: _____
Cost: _____ Delivery date & time: _____

❧ Ceremony

Bouquets
The bride: _____
_____ Cost: _____
Maid of honor: _____
_____ Cost: _____
Bridesmaids: _____ Cost per bouquet: _____
_____ Total cost: _____
Child attendants: _____ Cost per bouquet: _____
_____ Total cost: _____

Corsages
Mother of the bride: _____ Cost: _____
Mother of the groom: _____ Cost: _____
Other: _____ Cost: _____
Other: _____ Cost: _____
Other: _____ Cost: _____

Boutonnieres
Groom: _____ Cost: _____
Best man: _____ Cost: _____
Ushers: _____ Cost per boutonniere: _
_____ Total cost: _____
Father of the bride: _____ Cost: _____
Father of the groom: _____ Cost: _____
Other: _____ Cost: _____
Other: _____ Cost: _____

Music, Flowers, & Photography

FLOWERS

Decorative flowers: _____
_____
_____
_____ Cost: _____

❧ Reception

Centerpieces: _____
_____ Cost per centerpiece: _____
_____ Total cost: _____

Decorative arrangements: _____
_____
_____ Cost: _____

The Meaning of Flowers

*T*hroughout history, each flower has been assigned its own meaning or message. In the eighteenth century a literal language of flowers called "Floriography" was invented and gained popularity. A young male suitor would carefully select the stems for a bouquet, knowing that upon receipt of the flowers, his young lady would seriously interpret their message. The following is a list of some popular wedding flowers and the qualities they represent.

Baby's Breath . . . . *Pure Heart*	Calla Lilies . . . . *Sophistication & seductiveness*
Daisies . . . . *Innocence*	Irises . . . . *Flirtation*
Ivy . . . . *Friendship*	Lavender . . . . *Good fortune*
Lilacs . . . . *Romance*	Mountain Laurel . . . . . *Ambition*
Myrtle . . . . *Love*	Plum Blossoms . . . . . . *Fidelity*
Primrose . . . . *Youth*	Red Roses . . . . *Passion & desire*
Rose . . . . *Promise for the future*	Snowdrops . . . . *Hope*
Sweet Peas . . . . *Birth*	Violets . . . . *Faithfulness*
White Ranunculus . . . . *Charm*	

Music, Flowers, & Photography

NOTES & ESTIMATES

Music, Flowers, & Photography

PHOTOGRAPHY

❥ Formal Portrait

Photographer: _____
Address: _____
Phone: _____ Fax: _____ E-mail: _____
Cost: _____ Time & date of sitting: _____
Photos delivery date: _____
Quantity & sizes of prints included: _____
Cost of additional prints: _____
Notes & estimates: _____
_____
_____
_____
_____
_____
_____

❥ Ceremony & Reception

Photographer: _____
Address: _____
Phone: _____ Fax: _____ E-mail: _____
Cost: _____ Time & date of sitting: _____
Photos delivery date: _____
Quantity & sizes of prints included: _____
Cost of additional prints: _____
Notes & estimates: _____
_____
_____
_____
_____
_____
_____

Music, Flowers, & Photography

Videography

Videographer: _____ Contact: _____
Address: _____
Phone: _____ Fax: _____ E-mail: _____
Time booked: _____
Cost: _____ Number of VHS copies included: _____
Cost per additional copy: _____ Delivery date: _____
Services included: _____
_____
_____
_____
_____
_____
_____

Notes & estimates: _____
_____
_____
_____
_____
_____
_____
_____
_____
_____
_____
_____
_____
_____
_____

CEREMONY & RECEPTION

Choosing your ceremony and reception locations are the decisions that will most determine the ambience of your wedding. You may visit a number of sites before you find the one that seems perfect. Once you've narrowed down the choices, there are a number of factors you should consider before making your final decision.

Ceremony Location

- How many people can the location seat comfortably?
- How much time does the rental agreement allow for?
- Is there a wedding or event booked immediately before or after yours?
- How early before the ceremony can you set up and decorate the location?
- Are there any restrictions on flash photography, noise levels, decorations, lit candles, or recorded music?
- Is there adequate electricity?
- Is there space for live music?
- Does the location provide or rent chairs or benches?
- Is there wheelchair accessibility?
- Is there room for a receiving line?
- Are there private rooms for the bride and groom to dress or wait?
- If the location is outdoors, is a sheltered option available in case of inclement weather?

Reception Location

- Does the location provide party rentals, such as tables, silverware, glassware, tablecloths, napkins, etc.? What is the cost?
- Does the location offer catering services? Do they require that a specific caterer be used? If so, what is the cost?
- Can the location provide flowers and/or decorations? What is the cost?
- Can the location provide an event planner? What is the cost?

- Are there any restrictions on flash photography, noise levels, decorations, or lit candles?
- Can the location provide or rent a dance floor? What is the cost?
- Is there adequate electricity?
- How many people can the location seat comfortably?
- Is there wheelchair accessibility?
- How much time does the rental agreement allow for?
- Is there an event booked immediately before or after yours?
- How early can you set up and decorate the location?

If all these questions are answered to your satisfaction, ask the venue to provide you with a written agreement before signing a deposit check. The location agreement should incorporate any restrictions, time constraints, and services included. This will help avoid any unpleasant surprises or disagreements on your wedding day that might interfere with the joy of the event.

The style and content of both your ceremony and your reception may also depend greatly on your religion, heritage, nationality, family customs, and personal taste. Those who are devoutly religious, for instance, may have certain ceremonies that must be followed. Cultural traditions may also be integrated into the ceremony and reception through music, dance, readings, or prayer.

If you elect to include toasts by family and friends during the reception, be certain to ask participants well in advance of your wedding day. This will keep the reception fluid and allow those who are toasting plenty of time to consider and prepare their thoughts. You may also wish to ask a friend or relative with a particular musical talent to perform a special song or piece of music.

♥ ♥ ♥ ♥ ♥

Ceremony & Reception

The Ceremony

❧ Location

Site: _____ Contact: _____
Address: _____
Phone: _____ Fax: _____ E-mail: _____
Time availability: _____
_____
_____

Time booked: _____
Location fee: _____
Rentals available (aisle runner, chairs, candles, etc.): _____
_____
_____

Rentals cost: _____
Restrictions: _____
_____
_____

❧ Officiant

Name: _____
Address: _____
Phone: _____ Fax: _____ E-mail: _____
Fee: _____
Time availability: _____
_____

Time booked: _____

The Outdoor Wedding

If you're having an outdoor wedding, be prepared with alternatives if faced with bad weather. If possible, arrange for the option to move the ceremony indoors or have a tent set up in a nearby area. At the least, make sure you have a suitable number of white umbrellas on hand for you and your guests.

Ceremony & Reception

Notes & Estimates

_____
_____
_____
_____
_____
_____
_____
_____
_____
_____
_____
_____
_____
_____
_____
_____
_____
_____
_____
_____
_____
_____
_____
_____
_____
_____
_____

The Officiant

A great way to personalize your wedding is to have a friend or family member act as your officiant. If you don't know anyone who is licensed to conduct a marriage ceremony, consider asking a friend or family member to co-officiate with the judge or cleric.

Use this space to draw a layout of the ceremony site.

Ceremony & Reception

The Ceremony

- Personal Vows

| Ceremony & Reception |

The Ceremony

- **The Service**

Ceremony & Reception

The Ceremony

❧ The Program

Program title: _____

Printed by: _____ Contact: _____

Address: _____

Phone: _____ Fax: _____ E-mail: _____

Quantity: _____ Cost: _____ Delivery Date: _____

Names of participants and their roles:

_____
_____
_____
_____
_____
_____
_____
_____
_____

Printed statement to your guests: _____

_____
_____
_____
_____
_____
_____
_____
_____
_____

The Program

The ceremony program outlines the events and participants in the wedding service. Traditionally, the program includes the name and title of all the attendants and wedding party members. Musical selections, as well as poems and songs being recited by loved ones, are listed in order of performance. A personal message or quotation from the bride and groom adds an intimate and romantic touch.

| Ceremony & Reception |

Notes

Ceremony & Reception

NOTES

___

The Vows

The content of your ceremony is a highly personal choice. Whether you prefer a traditional ceremony or one that's more original, your officiant is an excellent source of advice. He or she should be able to provide you with several sample texts to give you ideas. If you choose to pen your own vows, don't wait until the last minute. Write them at least two weeks before your wedding day to give you plenty of time to commit the words to memory.

Ceremony & Reception

The Reception

❦ Location

Site: _____ Contact: _____
Address: _____
Phone: _____ Fax: _____ E-mail: _____
Time availability: _____
_____
Time booked: _____
Location fee: _____
Restrictions: _____
_____
_____

Services & equipment available: _____
_____
_____
_____
_____
_____

Notes & estimates: _____
_____
_____
_____
_____
_____
_____
_____
_____

Ceremony & Reception

THE RECEPTION

❧ Rental Equipment

Rental service: _____ Contact: _____
Address: _____
Phone: _____ Fax: _____ E-mail: _____
Cost: _____ Delivery date & time: _____
Items ordered: _____
_____
_____
_____
_____
_____
_____
_____
_____
_____

Notes & estimates: _____
_____
_____
_____
_____
_____
_____

The Receiving Line

*I*n a customary receiving line, the members of the wedding party line up to greet the guests just after the ceremony as they exit down the aisle. The traditional order of the receiving line is as follows: mother of the bride, father of the bride, mother of the groom, father of the groom, bride, groom, maid of honor, best man, wedding attendants.

Ceremony & Reception

THE RECEPTION

❧ Tent & Lighting Rental

Tent rental company: _____ Contact: _____

Address: _____

Phone: _____ Fax: _____ E-mail: _____

Cost: _____ Delivery date & time: _____

Tent ordered: _____
_____

Other equipment ordered (dance floor, tent flaps, etc.): _____
_____
_____
_____

Lighting rental company: _____ Contact: _____

Address: _____

Phone: _____ Fax: _____ E-mail: _____

Cost: _____ Delivery date & time: _____

Equipment ordered: _____
_____
_____
_____

❧ Other Rentals

Rental company: _____ Contact: _____

Address: _____

Phone: _____ Fax: _____ E-mail: _____

Cost: _____ Delivery date & time: _____

Equipment ordered: _____
_____
_____
_____
_____

Ceremony & Reception

NOTES & ESTIMATES

_____
_____
_____
_____
_____
_____
_____
_____
_____
_____
_____
_____
_____
_____
_____
_____
_____
_____
_____
_____
_____
_____
_____
_____

Getting to the Reception

If your ceremony and reception are not located in the same place, take into consideration the distance between them. Guests should not have to travel more than fifteen to twenty minutes to get to the reception site. Detailed, easy-to-follow directions should be provided to guests ahead of time to avoid confusion.

| Ceremony & Reception |

The Reception

❧ Seating Arrangements

Table #1
1. _____
2. _____
3. _____
4. _____
5. _____
6. _____
7. _____
8. _____
9. _____
10. _____

Table #2
1. _____
2. _____
3. _____
4. _____
5. _____
6. _____
7. _____
8. _____
9. _____
10. _____

Table #3
1. _____
2. _____
3. _____
4. _____
5. _____
6. _____
7. _____
8. _____
9. _____
10. _____

Table #4
1. _____
2. _____
3. _____
4. _____
5. _____
6. _____
7. _____
8. _____
9. _____
10. _____

Table #5
1. _____
2. _____
3. _____
4. _____
5. _____
6. _____
7. _____
8. _____
9. _____
10. _____

Table #6
1. _____
2. _____
3. _____
4. _____
5. _____
6. _____
7. _____
8. _____
9. _____
10. _____

Ceremony & Reception

The Reception

❖ Seating Arrangements

Table #7
1. _____
2. _____
3. _____
4. _____
5. _____
6. _____
7. _____
8. _____
9. _____
10. _____

Table #8
1. _____
2. _____
3. _____
4. _____
5. _____
6. _____
7. _____
8. _____
9. _____
10. _____

Table #9
1. _____
2. _____
3. _____
4. _____
5. _____
6. _____
7. _____
8. _____
9. _____
10. _____

Table #10
1. _____
2. _____
3. _____
4. _____
5. _____
6. _____
7. _____
8. _____
9. _____
10. _____

Table #11
1. _____
2. _____
3. _____
4. _____
5. _____
6. _____
7. _____
8. _____
9. _____
10. _____

Table #12
1. _____
2. _____
3. _____
4. _____
5. _____
6. _____
7. _____
8. _____
9. _____
10. _____

| Ceremony & Reception |

The Reception

❖ Seating Arrangements

Table #13
1. _____
2. _____
3. _____
4. _____
5. _____
6. _____
7. _____
8. _____
9. _____
10. _____

Table #14
1. _____
2. _____
3. _____
4. _____
5. _____
6. _____
7. _____
8. _____
9. _____
10. _____

Table #15
1. _____
2. _____
3. _____
4. _____
5. _____
6. _____
7. _____
8. _____
9. _____
10. _____

Table #16
1. _____
2. _____
3. _____
4. _____
5. _____
6. _____
7. _____
8. _____
9. _____
10. _____

Table #17
1. _____
2. _____
3. _____
4. _____
5. _____
6. _____
7. _____
8. _____
9. _____
10. _____

Table #18
1. _____
2. _____
3. _____
4. _____
5. _____
6. _____
7. _____
8. _____
9. _____
10. _____

Use this space to sketch the table arrangement.

Use this space to sketch the table arrangement.

Ceremony & Reception

The Reception

❦ Catering

Caterer: _____ Contact: _____

Address: _____

Phone: _____ Fax: _____ E-mail: _____

Time & hours booked: _____

Cost per person: _____

Number of servers: _____ Cost per server: _____

Total cost: _____

❦ Menu

Hors d'oeuvres: _____

_____
_____
_____
_____

Appetizers: _____

_____
_____
_____
_____

Entrées: _____

_____
_____
_____
_____
_____

Desserts: _____

_____
_____
_____
_____

| *Ceremony & Reception* |

NOTES

___

Serving Your Guests

How many weddings have you attended where the line for the bar is twenty people long? To avoid gridlock, consider having champagne and wine served from trays by waiters circulating the room, and offer only liquor and soft drinks at the bar.

Ceremony & Reception

The Reception

❦ Beverages

Beverage supplier: _____ Contact: _____
Address: _____
Phone: _____ Fax: _____ E-mail: _____
Cost: _____
_____

Delivery date & time: _____
Return policy: _____
_____

Beverages ordered: _____
_____
_____
_____
_____
_____
_____

Beverage supplier: _____ Contact: _____
Address: _____
Phone: _____ Fax: _____ E-mail: _____
Cost: _____
_____

Delivery date & time: _____
Return policy: _____
_____

Beverages ordered: _____
_____
_____
_____
_____
_____
_____

|Ceremony & Reception|

The Reception

❧ The Wedding Cake

Baker: _____ Contact: _____
Address: _____
Phone: _____ Fax: _____ E-mail: _____
Cost: _____ Delivery date & time: _____
Description of cake: _____
_____
_____
_____
_____
_____
_____
_____

❧ The Groom's Cake

Baker: _____ Contact: _____
Address: _____
Phone: _____ Fax: _____ E-mail: _____
Cost: _____ Delivery date & time: _____
Description of cake: _____
_____
_____
_____
_____
_____

The Groom's Cake

*T*he groom's cake, though often omitted from modern weddings, is traditionally chocolate and somewhat smaller than the wedding cake. Custom dictates that the groom's cake is presented to the groom at the reception and then sliced into pieces that are individually boxed and given to each guest to take home.

| *Ceremony & Reception* |

NOTES

The Honeymoon

You've said the big "I do!" Now what? Time to begin the rest of your life together, and it all starts with the honeymoon, a blissful vacation where the two of you can leave all your cares behind and enjoy each other in some magical and utterly peaceful setting.

Traditionally, the groom plans the honeymoon, often keeping the destination a secret from his bride until the last moment. But if you opt for this very romantic custom, take a few precautions. Make sure the groom tells you about the climate and occasions for which you need to pack. Also make sure you are informed with enough time to shop for items not readily on hand, such as suntan lotion for a tropical honeymoon, thermal underwear for a ski honeymoon, or hiking boots for a more rugged honeymoon. Be certain that passports (and, if necessary, inoculations) are up-to-date if travel abroad is part of the surprise.

If you opt to plan your honeymoon together, select a location that meets both of your expectations for a tranquil and relaxing vacation. If you can take at least two weeks off, consider spending half your time at a location of the bride's choosing, and half at a location of the groom's—and have two honeymoons instead of one!

The post-wedding hours find many newlyweds in a state of blissful fatigue. So consider taking a day or two—or at least that special first night—to relax at a nearby hotel or a local bed & breakfast before you run off to the airport. You may also wish to use this opportunity to visit a little more with family and friends.

Try and plan your honeymoon as far in advance as possible. Not only will you save on airfare and travel costs, but also you'll save yourself from having to worry about yet one more thing as the wedding day nears. In fact, it is a good idea to pack your suitcases at least a few days ahead of time. Just store them in a closet and pull them out when you are ready to leave.

With each marriage comes just one honeymoon, so give it as much careful thought and consideration as possible. Use the following pages to help you plan ahead and prepare this perfect trip. Above all else, don't forget your camera! Just as you may organize a wedding photo album, consider making a honeymoon album, as well. It's a wonderful way to share your travels with loved ones and revisit your experiences together, keeping the memories of your trip vivid and alive.

♥ ♥ ♥ ♥ ♥

Now that you've taken your vows and pledged a lifetime of love together, it's time to start looking ahead. Celebrating different wedding anniversaries by exchanging certain kinds of gifts has long been a tradition.

1st Anniversary	Cotton	13th Anniversary	Lace
2nd Anniversary	Paper	14th Anniversary	Ivory
3rd Anniversary	Leather	15th Anniversary	Crystal
4th Anniversary	Flowers/Fruit	20th Anniversary	China
5th Anniversary	Wood	25th Anniversary	Silver
6th Anniversary	Sugar or Iron	30th Anniversary	Pearls
7th Anniversary	Wool/Copper	35th Anniversary	Coral/Jade
8th Anniversary	Bronze	40th Anniversary	Rubies
9th Anniversary	Pottery	45th Anniversary	Sapphires
10th Anniversary	Tin	50th Anniversary	Gold
11th Anniversary	Steel	55th Anniversary	Emeralds
12th Anniversary	Linen/Silk	60th Anniversary	Diamonds

Honeymoon

Personal Information
(Clip to carry with you, but store separately from other vital documents and valuables)

❧ Bride
Name: _____
Passport number: _____
Drivers license number: _____
Camera model number: _____

Credit Cards	Number	Expiration Date
_____	_____	_____
_____	_____	_____
_____	_____	_____

❧ Groom
Name: _____
Passport number: _____
Drivers license number: _____
Camera model number: _____

Credit Cards	Number	Expiration Date
_____	_____	_____
_____	_____	_____
_____	_____	_____

❧ Travelers checks numbers:
_____
_____
_____
_____

❧ Emergency numbers:

Name	Phone Number
_____	_____
_____	_____
_____	_____

Honeymoon

Itinerary

Travel Agent: _____ Contact: _____
Address: _____
Phone: _____ Fax: _____ E-mail: _____

❧ Travel Information

Destination: _____
Depart from: _____ Arrive at: _____
Flight number: _____ Confirmation #: _____ Cost: _____
Car rental agency: _____ Cost: _____
Pickup time & place: _____
Drop-off time & place: _____
Accommodations: _____
Room reserved: _____ Rates: _____
Check-in time: _____ Checkout time: _____
Places of interest: _____
_____
Notes: _____
_____

Destination: _____
Depart from: _____ Arrive at: _____
Flight number: _____ Confirmation #: _____ Cost: _____
Car rental agency: _____ Cost: _____
Pickup time & place: _____
Drop-off time & place: _____
Accommodations: _____
Room reserved: _____ Rates: _____
Check-in time: _____ Checkout time: _____
Places of interest: _____
_____
Notes: _____
_____

Honeymoon

Itinerary

Destination: _____
Depart from: _____ Arrive at: _____
Flight number: _____ Confirmation #: _____ Cost: _____
Car rental agency: _____ Cost: _____
Pickup time & place: _____
Drop-off time & place: _____
Accommodations: _____
Room reserved: _____ Rates: _____
Check-in time: _____ Checkout time: _____
Places of interest: _____
_____
Notes: _____
_____
_____
_____
_____

Destination: _____
Depart from: _____ Arrive at: _____
Flight number: _____ Confirmation #: _____ Cost: _____
Car rental agency: _____ Cost: _____
Pickup time & place: _____
Drop-off time & place: _____
Accommodations: _____
Room reserved: _____ Rates: _____
Check-in time: _____ Checkout time: _____
Places of interest: _____
_____
Notes: _____
_____
_____
_____

| *Honeymoon* |

PACKING LIST

🌂 Item   Check when packed

| Honeymoon |

Packing List

Item Check when packed

Honeymoon

NOTES

A Wedding Cake Tradition

Saving the top tier of your wedding cake to be eaten on your one-year anniversary is a long-standing tradition. Be sure to seal the layer in an airtight container and place in your freezer. When the time comes, let the cake thaw for a few hours before serving.